CELEBRITY SECRETS

FASHION DESIGNERS

CATH SENKER

PowerKiDS press

New York

Published in 2012 by The Rosen Publishing Group, Inc.
29 East 21st Street, New York, NY 10010

First Edition

Senior Editor: Camilla Lloyd
Designer: Stephen Prosser

Picture Acknowledgments: The author and publisher would like to thank the following for allowing their pictures to be reproduced in this publication: Cover and 13: Eric Ryan/Getty Images; WWD/Condé Nast/Corbis: 2, 8, 9; JUSTIN LANE/epa/Corbis: 4; Jazz Archiv/Vas/dpa/Corbis: 7; Reuters/Corbis: 11; BENOIT TESSIER/Reuters/Corbis: 14; LUCAS DOLEGA/epa/Corbis: 15; GRAHAM TIM/CORBIS SYGMA: 16; Piotr Redlinski/Corbis: 19; ALESSANDRO GAROFALO/Reuters/Corbis: 20; Daniel Dal Zennaro/epa/Corbis: 21; Rex Features Ltd: 10, 17, 18, 22 (all), 23 (all); stocklight/Shutterstock: 1 and 5; BMCL/Shutterstock: 6; Entertainment Press/Shutterstock: 12; Milos Luzanin/Shutterstock: 24.

Library of Congress Cataloging-in-Publication Data

Senker, Cath.
 Fashion designers / by Cath Senker. — 1st ed.
     p. cm. — (Celebrity secrets)
 Includes index.
 ISBN 978-1-4488-7036-3 (library binding) — ISBN 978-1-4488-7082-0 (pbk.)
— ISBN 978-1-4488-7083-7 (6-pack)
 1. Fashion designers—Juvenile literature. 2. Fashion design—Juvenile literature. I. Title.
 TT507.S426 2012
 746.9'2092—dc23

                                        2011029069

Manufactured in Malaysia

CPSIA Compliance Information: Batch #WW2102PK: For Further Information contact Rosen Publishing, New York, New York at 1-800-237-9932

Contents

Marc Jacobs

MIXING ART AND FASHION

Marc speaks at a fashion press conference in August 2010.

Marc Jacobs is a fan of contemporary (present-day) art. He owns works by David Hockney and Damien Hirst.

Stats!

Name: Marc Jacobs

Date of birth: April 9, 1963

Education: Marc graduated from the Parsons School of Design, in New York, in 1984.

Personal life: Marc has a history of drug and alcohol abuse but has cleaned up his act and now follows a strict diet and exercise regime.

Fashion houses: He launched Marc Jacobs in 1986 then worked for Perry Ellis (1989–1994). Marc relaunched his own line in 1994 and then became artistic director of Louis Vuitton (LV) in 1998. He still runs his own design company, too.

Style: Eccentric, ranging from clothing that inspired the Seattle grunge music scene in the early 1990s to ladylike women's collections and quirky bag designs for LV.

Famous clients: Sofia Coppola, Winona Ryder, Lil' Kim, Kanye West, Kate Bosworth, Mischa Barton, Victoria Beckham.

Awards: Multiple awards, including CFDA Menswear Designer of the Year (2002), Accessories Designer of the Year (2003), Women's Luxe Fragrance of the Year (2010), and CFDA Womenswear Designer of the Year (2010).

Life Story

At 15, Marc worked stocking shelves in Charivari, a stylish New York boutique, where he first met Perry Ellis. As a young man, he launched his own collection with his business partner Robert Duffy, but retail sales were disappointing. He produced the famous grunge look while working for Perry Ellis, but sales were poor, and he lost his job. His relaunch of Marc Jacobs was more successful. Naomi Campbell and Linda Evangelista modeled for free, and the collection took off. At Louis Vuitton, the luxury bag and shoe company, Marc developed the company's first ready-to-wear line and focused on accessories.

Marc Jacobs makes women's, men's, and children's wear, eyewear, homewear, shoes, handbags, and fragrances.

> **Every year Marc's coats and bags are in great demand.**

Questions and Answers

Q **Are your clothes to be reserved for special occasions or to be worn and enjoyed?**

A "I'm not interested in making stuff for museums; I want the clothes to be worn. I don't care if the girl sits on a curb in them after a party and they're destroyed. I have to believe that there's going to be a life for these things."

Marc Jacobs, *Harper's Bazaar*, September 2010

Q **Now that you're a great American designer, can you relax?**

A "No, the reality is that we [the company] have to prove ourselves over and over again. It's not like we've reached a certain point and we're on cruise control. You've got to work harder and harder each time, not only to maintain but to better yourself and improve."

Marc Jacobs, *Out*, August 2007

Marc has successfully updated LV's image from luggage maker to creator of fashionable clothing and accessories. He has collaborated with artists such as Takashi Murakami and Stephen Sprouse to make original handbags with brightly colored and graffiti-inspired designs. He has greatly increased LV's profits, while expanding his own collections, which sell in over 100 stores worldwide.

Jimmy Choo

THE LUXURY SHOE MAKER

Jimmy Choo attends a film premiere in London in 2010.

Stats!

Name: Jimmy Choo

Date of birth: 1961

Education: Jimmy graduated from Cordwainer's College, now part of the London College of Fashion, in 1983.

Personal life: Jimmy is married and has a daughter. He lives in London, England.

Fashion houses: Jimmy Choo Ready-To-Wear, launched 1996; Jimmy Choo Couture, 2001.

Style: Sophisticated, luxurious, and glamorous footwear.

Famous clients: Jennifer Lopez, Mary J. Blige, Sandra Bullock, Jennifer Aniston.

Awards: Jimmy Choo's recent awards include ACE Designer Brand of the Year award (2008), British Designer Brand of the Year Award from the British Fashion Council (2008), Footwear News Brand of the Year Award (2008), and the 2009 Nordstrom Partners In Excellence award.

Jimmy Choo's collection for H&M in 2009 resulted in 12-hour lines outside the branch on Oxford Street, in London!

Life Story

Jimmy Choo was born into a family of shoemakers and made his first shoe when he was just 11 years old. After working as an apprentice in the family business for several years, in 1980 he moved to London, England and went to college. In 1986, he opened his own shoemaking workshop in East London,

Questions and Answers

Q **What keeps you awake at night?**

A "I love my work so much I can never switch off when I go home. I am constantly thinking of ways to improve."

Jimmy Choo, University of the Arts London Web site, 2010

Q **What's your advice to would-be shoe designers?**

A "So many designers talk about the 'concept,' but unless you can realize the concept into a product, it's meaningless. So the message is you need to know the traditional skills as well. Unless you have skills, 'concept' is meaningless."

Jimmy Choo, *Berkshire Life*, April 2010

making top-quality designer shoes by hand. *Vogue* accessories editor Tamara Mellon was passionate about Choo's shoes and owned countless pairs. The daughter of Tom Yeardye (the wealthy businessman who had co-founded the Vidal Sassoon hair empire), Tamara visited Jimmy Choo's workshop and proposed a business partnership. In 1996, Mellon and Choo set up Jimmy Choo Ltd. Tamara found factories in Italy to produce the shoes, and Jimmy Choo Ready-To-Wear was born. In 2001 Jimmy Choo returned to producing glamorous handmade shoes under the Jimmy Choo Couture line, ending his involvement in the ready-to-wear line.

The ready-to-wear line has since expanded and produces boots, shoes, sneakers, handbags, and accessories. There are over 100 Jimmy Choo stores worldwide.

Jennifer Aniston wearing Jimmy Choos to *The Bounty Hunter* premiere in 2010.

Jimmy Choo achieved success by expanding the business with Tamara and becoming a worldwide fashion name. Yet he preferred to return to creating handmade shoes for individuals rather than producing large-scale collections.

7

Miuccia Prada

THE INTELLECTUAL DESIGNER

Miuccia attends the Costume Institute Gala at the Metropolitan Museum of Art in 2010.

The 2006 film *The Devil Wears Prada* showed the stress of working for a top fashion magazine. The actors wore a variety of designer clothes—including Prada, of course!

Stats!

Name: Miuccia Prada

Date of birth: May 10, 1949

Education: Miuccia obtained a PhD in political science from the University of Milan and studied mime for five years.

Personal life: Miuccia married Patrizio Bertelli in 1987 and they have two sons. The couple is passionate about contemporary art and launched the Prada Foundation in 1993 to support it.

Fashion houses: In 1978, Miuccia and her husband took over the running of Prada, the family business. She launched her own offshoot line, Miu Miu, in 1992.

Style: Casual, understated luxury. Miuccia's clothes are cool, comfortable, and minimalist. She often pairs the more traditional clothes with exciting and modern clothes and can even make a parka look cool!

Famous clients: Tilda Swinton, Charlize Theron, Debra Messing, Kate Bosworth, Vanessa Traina.

Awards: Council of Fashion Designers of America (CFDA) International Award (1993), Footwear Designer of the Year (1996), Special Achievement award National Italian American Foundation (2000), McKim Medal for contribution to the arts (2010).

Life Story

Miuccia grew up in Milan, Italy. Her parents ran Prada, a leather goods company that had been founded by Miuccia's grandfather. Miuccia did not study fashion design and was reluctant to take over the business, although she did join in the 1970s to supervise the design of accessories.

Miuccia went into partnership with Patrizio in 1978, and the pair took over the control of Prada. They moved into fashion-led style, launching women's wear (1988), menswear (1994), and Prada Sport (1997). The company also produces eyewear, cosmetics, fragrances, shoes, and handbags.

One of Miuccia's first designs was a black nylon bag, made with a fabric used to make military tents. It was followed by a ready-to-wear line using the same fabric. Her notion of casual luxury caught on, and in the 1990s the brand gained a cult following. Miuccia has an unusual sense of fashion. Her clothes sometimes even look frumpy. Yet they are unique and desirable. It's said that Miuccia designs for women's brains rather than their bodies, meaning that her clothes are easy to wear and stylish.

A model in an outfit from the 2009 Miu Miu ready-to-wear collection.

Questions and Answers

Q How important is fashion?

A "I love fashion, but I think it should stay in its place, not rule your life. It's a very nice part of your life, but I think it should be fun."

Miuccia Prada, *Vogue UK*, April 2008

Q You and your husband Patrizio are known for your violent arguments. How do you manage to work together?

A "We work hard. It's always an intense relationship, and it's exhausting having to work with him. But I admire and respect him. It's a war in here every minute, and to be part of this company, you have to be trained."

Miuccia Prada, *Fashionologie*, March 12, 2010

Tom Ford

CLASSIC MENSWEAR DESIGNER

Tom attends a charity gala in May 2010.

Tom Ford loves filmmaking. His first movie, *A Single Man*, debuted in 2009 and had excellent reviews. The film was nominated for an Oscar.

Stats!

Name: Tom Ford

Date of birth: August 27, 1962

Education: Tom graduated from the Parsons School of Design, in New York, in 1986.

Personal life: Tom lives with his long-term partner, Richard Buckley. He has a villa in Los Angeles, a ranch house in New Mexico, and a town house in London, England.

Fashion houses: During the late 1980s, Tom worked for Perry Ellis and Cathy Hardwick in New York. In 1990 he moved to Gucci in Italy. When Gucci bought a share of Yves Saint Laurent he was made creative director of their ready-to-wear lines. In 2005 he set up his own fashion empire, Tom Ford.

Style: Designer classics—high-quality, slim-fitting dark suits with crisp white shirts, worn with one or two accessories.

Famous clients: Johnny Depp, Tom Hanks, Bradley Cooper, Pierce Brosnan, Jon Hamm, Daniel Craig.

Awards: ACE Award for an accessory brand launch (2006), CFDA Menswear Designer of the Year (2008), and GQ Germany Man of the Year (2009).

Life Story

Tom moved from Austin, Texas when he was 17 to study art history at New York University, but he dropped out after a year and switched to studying interior design. In the evenings he went clubbing. The glamorous disco wear he saw would later influence his Gucci designs. After working for a few years in New York, he decided that he needed to experience European fashion

design, which prompted his move to Gucci in Milan, Italy. At Gucci, he created several series of mostly 1970s-inspired women's and men's collections. His creations proved extremely popular, and Gucci's profits rose.

Tom left Gucci to set up his own company, Tom Ford, which creates menswear, beauty products, eyewear, and accessories. He opened his first store in New York in 2007; other stores around the world followed. Tom is hardworking, has good business sense, and has a keen eye for designs that will sell. His new womenswear line, eagerly awaited by the fashion world, launched in 2011. Tom is also developing his career as a filmmaker and owns his own production company.

A model presents one of Tom Ford's creations for fashion house Yves Saint Laurent, in 2010.

Stella McCartney

ECO-CONSCIOUS BOHEMIAN FASHIONS

Stella attends a party at the Stella McCartney store in 2008.

Stats!

Name: Stella McCartney

Date of birth: September 13, 1971

Education: Graduated from Central Saint Martins College of Art and Design in London, in 1995.

Personal life: In 2003 Stella married Alasdhair Willis; they have four children. She cares passionately about animal rights and is a vegetarian.

Fashion houses: Stella was the creative director for Chloé, in Paris (1997–2001) and established her own fashion label in partnership with Gucci in 2001.

Style: Bohemian, feminine styles.

Famous clients: Madonna, Kate Moss, Cameron Diaz, Gwyneth Paltrow.

Awards: Stella's many awards include British Designer of the Year British Fashion Awards (2007) and Green Designer of the Year at the Accessories Council Excellence (ACE) Awards, New York, (2008).

Stella McCartney doesn't use leather or fur in her designs. The company is eco-conscious. It recycles around 2 tons (2 t) of paper a year and makes 100 percent biodegradable bags from corn.

Life Story

Stella is the daughter of famous rock star Paul McCartney and animal rights activist Linda McCartney. Stella always loved clothes. When she was just 15 years old, she went to work with French designer Christian Lacroix. Her graduation show collection was a hit in U.S. stores. Stella's big break came when she was appointed director of Chloé in 1997.

Stella poses with models at the Stella McCartney ready-to-wear show in Paris 2009.

Stella's collections include women's ready-to-wear, accessories, lingerie, eyewear, fragrance, and organic skincare. She has taken part in many joint ventures with companies such as H&M and Gap.

People have sometimes said that she has risen to the top simply because of her famous parents, but Stella is a savvy designer who has successfully combined haute couture with high-street fashion. Her 2005 collection for H&M sold out in minutes!

Questions and Answers

Q **What do you mean when you say your company is cruelty free?**

A "Everything in my store and every single garment and accessory that you see is cruelty free, in the sense that no animal has died to make anything in here. A lot of people out there don't want products that an animal has had to die for."

Stella McCartney, stellamccartney.com, 2010

Q **Do you think it's acceptable for people to wear items from your collection with non-designer items?**

A "I think it is good that there is so much choice out there and that people are really making their own decisions. When I design it is all about you can take this top and you can put it with any trousers or if you want you can wear this skirt with any old top, it could be from the charity shop, it could be your grandmother's, it doesn't matter. That is the way I design because that is the way I dress."

Stella McCartney, *Elle Canada*, May 2009

Yohji Yamamoto

EAST-MEETS-WEST FASHIONS

Yohji at a ready-to-wear show during Paris Fashion Week, 2010.

Yohji Yamamoto is a karate expert, who has his own *dojo*, a martial arts exercise hall, in his Tokyo home.

Stats!

Name: Yohji Yamamoto

Date of birth: October 3, 1943

Education: Yohji obtained a degree in law in 1966 and a degree in fashion design from Bunka Fashion College, in Tokyo, Japan, in 1969.

Personal life: Yohji likes to keep his personal life private. It is known he had a relationship with Rei Kawakubo, another avant-garde Japanese designer, in the late 1980s and early 1990s. He has a daughter, Limi Feu, who is also a fashion designer.

Fashion house: Yohji Yamamoto.

Style: Avant-garde. Loose, unstructured clothing that flows with the wearer's movement. The clothes are often black, with occasional splashes of color. Yamamoto combines the traditional Japanese kimono style with modern ready-to-wear Western fashion.

Famous clients: Donna Karan, Gwen Stefani, Elton John.

Awards: Yohji Yamamoto's awards include the Japanese Medal of Honor (2004) and Honorary Royal Designer for Industry from the Royal Society of Arts (2006).

Life Story

Yamamoto was raised in Japan by his mother, who sewed clothes for a living. After graduating with a degree in fashion design, he launched Y's in 1972, a women's ready-to-wear label, and presented his first collection in Tokyo in 1977. Yohji made his debut in Paris in 1981 and launched Yohji Yamamoto. He received enthusiastic praise for his unusual loose garments, which were so different from the power suits and stilettos of the time.

Yohji's designs at Men's Fashion Week in Paris, 2010.

Questions and Answers

Q   How do you go about making a garment?

A   "Making a garment means thinking about people. I am always eager to meet people and talk to them. It's what I like more than anything else. What are they doing? What are they thinking? How do they lead their lives? And then I can set to work. I start with the fabric, the actual material, the "feel" of it. I then move on to the form. Possibly what counts most for me is the feel. And then, when I start working on the material, I think my way into the form it ought to assume."

Yohji Yamomoto, *Radical Elegance*, Art Gallery of Western Australia, 2007

Q   Did you ever imagine you would one day own an international fashion empire?

A   "No. All I ever really wanted to do in my life was to spend each day quietly in the studio making clothes."

Yohji Yamamoto, *New York Times*, October 2009

His main ready-to-wear lines include Yohji Yamamoto, Yohji Yamamoto pour homme (for men), and Yohji Yamamoto + Noir. Y's is his less expensive line. He has collaborated with other fashion brands, such as Adidas and Hermès. In 2006 he began to design luggage and accessories for an Italian company, Mandarina Duck.

Yohji Yamamoto has made a name for himself internationally, with shops in Paris, London, and various Japanese cities. An extremely hardworking designer, he creates multiple fresh designs for different brands each year.

Paul Smith

CLASSIC DESIGNS WITH A TWIST

Paul Smith at a fashion show in aid of Macmillan Cancer Relief.

Stats!

Name: Paul Smith

Date of birth: July 5, 1946

Education: Paul left school at the age of 15 without graduating.

Personal life: Paul lives with his long-term partner, Pauline Denyer.

Fashion house: Paul Smith.

Style: Classic British tailoring with a clever twist. He combines garments in an unusual way and adds contrasting colors and quirky design details.

Famous clients: Parker Posey, Mick Jagger, David Bowie, Jack Nicholson, George Michael, Matthew McConaughey.

Awards: Paul Smith was knighted in 2000 for his services to the fashion industry. He won the Queen's Award for Enterprise in 2009 and was nominated for Best Menswear Designer in 2010.

In 2009, Paul Smith designed a special Champions League final suit for Manchester United football (soccer) team.

Life Story

As a teenager, Paul wanted to be a professional cyclist, but his hopes were dashed when he had a terrible accident at 17. After recovering, he made friends with some art students and decided to enter the exciting world of fashion. He attended evening classes in tailoring, and with the help of his fashion-graduate girlfriend Pauline Denyer, he opened a tiny boutique in 1970. In 1976 he exhibited his first menswear collection in Paris under his own label. Over the next two decades he rose to become a top British designer.

Paul Smith has 12 collections, including menswear, womenswear, accessories, shoes, fragrances, and furniture. The company has even gone global. His products are sold in 35 countries and are particularly popular in Japan, where he has more than 200 stores. His good business sense and instinct for upcoming trends enabled him to build his fashion empire. Paul is seen as a modest, down-to-earth man who stays involved in the day-to-day running of the business. He is the chairman of the company, but he still designs the clothes and visits his stores.

Questions and Answers

Q   How would you describe your style?

A "A lot of the things from the outside are very simple and easy to wear but on the inside you discover brightly colored lining or button holes that are purple or every button which is different, so it's always got a sense of humor."

Paul Smith, designboom.com, February 2010

Q   What's your advice to aspiring fashion designers?

A "Well just remember that in any form of creative business there are a lot of people out there doing the same job so you've got to have a reason to be. One of the best ways to understand that is through experience, so as a fashion designer try and get a Saturday job in a boutique or work placement because living in the real world as opposed to just drawing makes you understand that it's not just about design but much more."

Paul Smith, *Impact*, October 2009

Kate and Laura Mulleavy

ROMANTIC, FEMININE STYLES

Kate and Laura attend a private dinner to celebrate the launch of Rodarte at Harvey Nichols, 2009.

Stats!

Name: Kate and Laura Mulleavy

Dates of birth: Kate Mulleavy was born on February 11, 1979; Laura Mulleavy was born on August 31, 1980

Education: Kate studied art history while Laura studied literature. They both graduated with a degree from the University of California, Berkeley in 2001. The sisters have no formal fashion training.

Personal life: Kate and Laura live at home with their parents and work together in Los Angeles.

Fashion house: Rodarte.

Style: Romantic, flowing, feminine styles with intricate details.

Famous clients: Cate Blanchett, Natalie Portman, Keira Knightley, Emma Watson, Kirsten Dunst, Michelle Obama, Reese Witherspoon, Chloe Sevigny, Tilda Swinton, Dita von Teese.

Awards: CFDA Swarovski Emerging Womenswear Designer award (2008), Swiss Textiles Award (2008), CFDA Womenswear Designer of the Year (2009).

Kate and Laura like to link their shows to movies. One season, they were inspired by Japanese horror films and presented dresses complete with slashes and bloodstains.

Life Story

Kate and Laura were always fascinated by clothing design. After graduating from college, they returned home and began to make clothes. In 2005 they launched Rodarte, presenting their first collection of ten garments during New York Fashion Week. They met with immediate success, appearing on the cover of *Women's Wear Daily* and meeting with *Vogue* editor Anna Wintour. Key retailers such as Bergdorf Goodman and Barneys decided to stock their collection.

Questions and Answers

Q You and Laura are inseparable. What are the benefits of working with someone so close to you?

A "When you have a creative relationship with someone like Laura, you don't have to go to other people to hear what they think. You have each other. One day you love an idea, and the next day you can't stand it. There's a lot of insecurity in designing, and what helps me is that Laura and I can get lost together."

Kate Mulleavy, *Wall Street Journal*, March 2009

Q How do you find inspiration?

A "Inspiration can come from anywhere. Movies, art, stuff we see day-to-day. Like, the other day we were on the highway and we saw a car that was half blue, half white. It was really odd; something you'd definitely notice. And at the time, we happened to be in the middle of an argument about color, and that car kind of settled it, right there. Blue."

Laura Mulleavy, Style File blog, December 2008

The Rodarte Fashion Show at Olympus Fashion Week, 2007.

Rodarte makes womenswear, handbags, and clothes and has collaborated with Gap and Target GO International. Kate and Laura have risen rapidly to fame owing to their dogged determination to make it in the fashion world, the appeal of their beautiful, romantic dresses, and the strong working relationship they have.

19

Dolce and Gabbana

ITALIAN LUXURY

Dolce and Gabbana acknowledge the applause at the Fall Women's Collection in Milan in 2010.

Stats!

Names: Domenico Dolce and Stefano Gabbana

Date of birth: Domenico Dolce was born on August 13, 1958; Stefano Gabbana was born on November 14, 1962

Education: Domenico studied fashion design in Sicily, Italy, while Stefano studied graphic design in Milan, Italy.

Personal life: Domenico and Stefano used to be a couple. They broke up in 2005 but continued their business partnership.

Fashion house: Dolce & Gabbana.

Style: For women, clothes designed to emphasize their curves; for men, a combination of fine, tailored suits and casual clothes.

Famous clients: Madonna, Monica Bellucci, Isabella Rosellini, Kylie Minogue, Angelina Jolie, David and Victoria Beckham, Katy Perry.

Awards: Best Designer of the Year Award in New York (2003), Best International Designers by British *Elle* readers (2004), Lead award for Best Advertising Campaign of the Year (2006).

Dolce and Gabbana often use soccer players in their advertisements to appeal to male customers. One advertisement showed top Italian players in their underwear!

Life Story

Domenico gained experience in his parents' businesses. His father was a tailor and his mother ran a clothing store. Stefano gained work experience in the fashion industry as an assistant in a Milan studio, where the pair met in 1980. They began taking on freelance design work together in 1982, and in 1986 they burst onto the fashion scene with their first women's collection in Milan, to rave reviews. The company expanded in the late 1980s. In 1989 they opened their first boutique in Japan and soon afterward, in New York.

Dolce and Gabbana at the Summer Women's ready-to-wear show, 2005.

Dolce & Gabbana is now a leading luxury goods company, producing not only clothing but also leather goods, footwear, and accessories under two main brands. Dolce & Gabbana focuses on classics rather than seasonal fashions. D&G is the younger, more casual line. Dolce & Gabbana has been described as a "lifestyle brand" rather than simply a fashion company. International fashion editors, buyers, and A-list celebrities line up to attend their shows.

Questions and Answers

Q How do you know if your ideas will sell?

A "The question that we ask ourselves every day is: are our ideas in line with the rest of the world? This is the most important thing. It is not necessary to be too avant-garde, because you risk not being understood. You need to be ahead of the game just enough so that you can have what people want in the shops when they want it."

Domenico Dolce, *Guardian*, June 2010

Q Do you mind when people mimic your designs?

A "It's always a pleasure for us to walk along the street and see young men and women dressed in a Dolce & Gabbana or D&G style despite the fact that they don't own a single item of clothing from either. It means that the message we wanted to convey has been passed on and understood."

Stefano Gabbana, *The Independent*, March 2010

OTHER FASHION DESIGNERS

Matthew Williamson

Basic Information

Home: Born in Manchester, England. Lives in London.

Birthday: October 23, 1971

Career

Background: Matthew graduated from Central Saint Martins College of Art and Design in 1994.

Career: After working for Monsoon and Accessorize, Matthew set up his own company in 1997 and quickly established his reputation as a designer. From 2005–2008, he also worked as Creative Director at Italian fashion house Pucci.

Style: Colorful, vibrant boho-style party and holiday wear, sometimes with an Indian influence.

Famous designs: Kaleidoscopic dress prints.

Interests: Matthew loves spending time with his celebrity friends, who include Sienna Miller and Helena Christensen.

Web site: www.matthewwilliamson.com

Junya Watanabe

Basic Information

Home: Born in Tokyo, Japan, where he still lives.

Birthday: 1961

Career

Background: Junya attended Bunka College of Fashion in Tokyo, Japan, graduating in 1984.

Career: Upon graduation, Junya went to work for Comme des Garçons. After eight years, he started his own womenswear line under the Comme des Garçons label. In 2000 he debuted a men's line.

Style: Junya produces radical fashion. He uses inventive layering and draping and places seams and zippers in unusual places.

Famous designs: Dresses and blouses made from glow-in-the-dark fabric.

Interests: Junya is interested in "techno couture," which he calls "Science Non-Fiction." He uses futuristic, cutting-edge fabrics.

Philip Treacy

Basic Information

Home: Born in County Galway, Ireland. Lives in London.

Birthday: May 26, 1967

Career

Background: Philip studied fashion at the National College of Art and Design in Dublin, Ireland, and then at the Royal College of Art in London, receiving an MA in 1990.

Career: Upon graduation, Philip established his own company making sensational hats and also collaborated with Karl Lagerfeld of Chanel. He has designed hats for several haute-couture houses, and his creations are extremely popular with the women of the British royal family.

Style: Extraordinary, eye-catching hats.

Famous designs: The first hat Philip designed for Chanel was a twisted birdcage, worn on the cover of British *Vogue* by Linda Evangelista.

Interests: Philip has designed for ballet, films, and theater productions. He loves photography.

Web site: www.philiptreacy.co.uk

Alexander McQueen

Career

Background: Alexander worked for several tailors and designers before attending Central Saint Martins College of Art and Design (1990–1992).

Career: In 1992 Alexander's low-slung pants brought him instant fame. In 1996 he became head designer of French fashion house Givenchy. He left in 2001 and expanded his brand to include fragrances and menswear. Tragically, Alexander committed suicide in 2010.

Style: Theatrical, adventurous fashions.

Famous designs: "Bumsters," which are pants cut so low at the back that they reveal the cleavage of the backside!

Interests: Alexander was a skilled scuba diver.

Web site: www.alexandermcqueen.com

Basic Information

Home: Born in London. Found dead in London on February 11, 2010.

Birthday: March 17, 1969

Katharine Hamnett

Career

Background: Katharine studied fashion in Sweden and then at Central Saint Martins College of Art and Design, graduating in 1969.

Career: She set up her own fashion business with a college friend and then launched the Katharine Hamnett label in 1979, which achieved rapid success.

Style: Katharine invented block-printed T-shirts with slogans.

Famous designs: In 2003, after the U.S.-led invasion of Iraq, Katharine produced "Stop the War" T-shirts for London Fashion Week.

Interests: Katharine campaigns against injustice and for the protection of the environment. She insists on producing her clothes in ethical and environmentally-friendly ways, for example, by using organic cotton.

Web site: www.katharinehamnett.com

Basic Information

Home: Born in Gravesend, Kent, England. Lives in London.

Birthday: August 16, 1947

Christopher Kane

Career

Background: While studying at Central Saint Martins College of Art and Design, Christopher worked part-time for fashion designers. He graduated in 2006.

Career: Christopher won an award for his MA graduate collection and was immediately taken on by Versace as a consultant. He also established his own label in 2006 with his sister Tammy, and his collections went from strength to strength.

Style: Avant-garde, edgy designs.

Famous designs: Christopher's spring 2007 debut collection included super-short neon bandage dresses.

Interests: Christopher loves to promote his home country and in 2008 was appointed ambassador for Visit Scotland, the national tourism organization of Scotland.

Basic Information

Home: Born in Glasgow, Scotland. Lives in London.

Birthday: July 26, 1982

Glossary

accessories (ik-SEH-soh-rees) Things that are not necessary, but add beauty or convenience. In fashion, these can be things such as hats, scarves, or jewelry pieces.

apprentice (uh-PREN-tis) A person who learns a trade by working for someone who is already trained.

boutique (boo-TEEK) A small store that sells very specialized merchandise.

clients (KLY-ents) People who pay a company or other people to do something.

collaborate (kuh-LA-buh-rayt) To work jointly toward a common goal.

garments (GAR-ments) Items of clothing.

luxurious (lug-ZHOOR-ee-us) Very comfortable and beautiful.

Index

Web Sites

Due to the changing nature of Internet links, PowerKids Press has developed an online list of Web sites related to the subject of this book. This site is updated regularly. Please use this link to access the list:
www.powerkidslinks.com/celeb/fashion/